# bread &
# muffin
## *perfection*

HINKLER
BOOKS

# bread &
# muffin
## *perfection*

Food Editor
**Jody Vassallo**

Creative Director
**Sam Grimmer**

Project Editor
**Lara Morcombe**

**HB**
HINKLER
BOOKS

First published in 2004 by Hinkler Books Pty Ltd
45–55 Fairchild Street
Heatherton Victoria Australia 3202
www.hinklerbooks.com

10 9 8 7 6

10 09 08

Disclaimer: The nutritional information listed under each recipe does not include the nutrient content of garnishes or
any accompaniments not listed in specific quantitites in the ingredient list. The nutritional information for each recipe
is an estimate only, and may vary depending on the brand of ingredients used, and due to natural biological variations
in the composition of natural foods such as meat, fish, fruit and vegetables. The nutritional information was calculated
by using Foodworks dietary analysis software (Version 3, Xyris Software Pty Ltd, Highgate Hill, Queensland, Australia)
based on the Australian food composition tables and food manufacturers' data. Where not specified, ingredients are
always analysed as average or medium, not small or large.

ISBN: 978-1-8651-5772-6

Printed and bound in China

# contents

# an introduction to bread & muffins

Cheese and bacon muffins offer a fresh interpretation of a classic breakfast, lemon currant muffins are perfect with a cup of warm tea, and blue cheese and walnut damper adds a rustic touch to a dinner party menu. Quick breads range from muffins, scones and hot cross buns to croissants, banana bread and gingerbread people. What they all have in common is that they are cooked without yeast, they rarely require kneading and they are quick and easy to make.

## quick breads

The whole process of making quick breads can take less time than it would for you to jump into a car and shop for pre-made breads at your local supermarket. It can be as simple as sifting together a few dry ingredients, whisking some eggs, butter and liquid, gently combining the lot, pouring the batter into muffin pans, whacking it in the oven and waiting until cooked.

Quick breads can be cooked in muffin tins, on baking trays or in loaf tins. The size of the loaf tin will not make that much difference. If the tin is larger than the one suggested in the recipe, the cooking time will be shorter. Take care, however, not to try to cook it in a smaller tin as the bread needs room to rise and if the tin is too small the batter will spill over the side of the tin. Cook quick breads until a skewer inserted into the center comes out clean.

There are three main methods for preparing quick bread mixtures:

1 Muffin method – see the Muffins section later.

2 Scone method – which involves rubbing cold butter into the dry ingredients until the mixture resembles coarse breadcrumbs before stirring in the liquid and mixing it to form a soft dough.

3 Creaming method – beating butter and sugar with electric beaters until light and fluffy, then gradually adding the eggs, followed by a portion of the dry ingredients folded in with a portion of the liquid ingredients. The creaming method produces a finer more cake like textured quick bread as the emphasis is on adding air to the mixture.

## muffins

First thing you will need to do before you start is to preheat your oven. Muffins are usually cooked on a slightly higher temperature than cakes so check the recipe, but as a rough guide it is likely you will be cooking at 200°C (400°F, gas mark 6).

Check the recommended tin size. Don't panic if you do not have the exact size – this usually means that you will end up with more or less muffins. Non-stick muffin tins come in a variety of sizes. The most popular are: 1 cup (Texas muffin) tin with 6 holes; 1/2 cup tin with 12 holes; 1/3 cup tin with 12 holes; and mini muffin tins with 12 holes. The easiest way to measure the capacity of a tin is to measure out 1 cup (250 ml, 8 fl oz) water in a jug and pour it into a hole until it reaches the top. If you are planning to line the holes with paper cases do this before you start preparing the mixture. If the paper cases are thin you may want to use a double layer to help them sit in place.

Now it is time to read the recipe and measure out the ingredients. Sift the flour and dry ingredients into a large bowl that has enough room for the ingredients to be mixed together without spilling any over the side. Make a well in the center of the dry ingredients; this will give you a place into which you can pour the liquid ingredients. Set this bowl aside while you whisk together the wet mixture. This is best done in a jug as it makes pouring easier. Whisk the ingredients together either with a small whisk or fork until well combined – this is quite important as they are only gently stirred through the dry ingredients and unbeaten egg can be a problem.

Now pour all of the liquid into the well and fold them together using either a large spatula or metal spoon. It is very important not to over mix the batter – it should still be quite lumpy. If you over beat a muffin batter you will find yourself with bouncy rubbery muffins rather than lightly textured moist ones. Spoon the mixture into the prepared holes, only fill the holes to three quarters full as muffins need room to rise and peak at the top.

Place the muffins on the middle shelf of the preheated oven. Cook for the specified recipe time but check about 5 minutes before the end of cooking as fan-forced ovens can be hotter and cook faster than normal convection ovens. You may also need to turn the tin during cooking if the back of your oven is hotter than the front.

There are a couple of ways to test whether a muffin is cooked. Often you will be able to see that the muffin has started to come away from the side of the tin. Otherwise, insert a skewer into the center of the muffin and if it comes out clean it is cooked.

Allow the muffins to cool in the tin for about 5 minutes before turning out onto a wire rack to cool completely or eat warm with some butter and a cup of coffee.

## basic sweet muffin recipe

300 g (10 oz) self-rising flour
125 g (4 oz) castor sugar
1 1/2 cups (375 ml, 12 fl oz) buttermilk
2 eggs
150 g (5 oz) butter, melted and cooled slightly

1 Preheat oven to 200°C (400°F, gas mark 6). Sift flour into a bowl and stir in sugar. Make a well in the centre.

2 Whisk together the buttermilk, eggs and butter. Pour into the dry ingredients and mix gently until the mixture is just combined.

3 Spoon the mixture into 12 of the 1/2-cup capacity muffins holes and bake for 20–25 minutes or until risen and golden and starting to come away from the side of the tin.

Note: For a basic savoury muffin recipe, delete the sugar.

### storage
Cooled cooked muffins can be stored at room temperature in an air-tight container for 2–3 days. Frozen muffins can be stored in plastic wrap or a freezer bag for up to 3 months. Thaw at room temperature or in the microwave on defrost.

## scones

There are a couple of simple tips that will help you when making scones. Firstly, use cold butter to rub into the flour. You can either cut the butter into the flour using a flat bladed knife or you can rub the butter in using your fingertips. Whatever you decide, work quickly.

Make a well in the center and pour in the liquid. Mix the ingredients together using a flat bladed knife; the mixture should come together in clumps. Remember it is better to add liquid to the mixture rather than flour. Gather the dough together with your hands and turn it out on a lightly floured surface.

Scones should not be kneaded, as this will make the dough tough and heavy. Pat or roll out the dough and use a lightly floured cutter to remove rounds of the dough. Place the scones close, but not touching, onto a baking tray lined with baking paper or lightly greased. Brush the tops with milk as this gives them a golden top as they bake.

Checking scones for readiness is tricky. Probably the best way is to break a scone open to see if it is light and fluffy inside. If it is still moist and slightly wet, cook the scones for a little longer.

If you prefer soft topped scones to those with a crisper top, wrap the warm scones in a clean tea towel and allow them to cool slightly.

# muffins

# cornbread muffins

## ingredients

185 g (6 oz) self-raising flour
170 g (5$\frac{1}{2}$ oz) polenta
45 g (1$\frac{1}{2}$ oz) parmesan, grated
1 teaspoon baking powder
1 teaspoon ground cumin
pinch chilli powder
2 cups (500 ml, 16 fl oz) buttermilk
  or low-fat milk
2 eggs, lightly beaten
1 tablespoon vegetable oil
**makes 12**

**i**

**preparation time**
15 minutes

**cooking time**
30 minutes

**nutritional value
per serve**
fat: 4.6 g
carbohydrate: 27 g
protein: 8.7 g

**1** Preheat oven to 190°C (375°F, gas mark 5). In a large bowl, combine flour, polenta, parmesan, baking powder, cumin and chilli powder.

**2** Make a well in centre of flour mixture, add milk, eggs and oil and mix until just combined.

**3** Spoon mixture into 12 greased $\frac{1}{3}$ cup (90 ml, 3 fl oz) capacity muffin tins and bake for 30 minutes or until muffins are cooked when tested with a skewer. Turn onto a wire rack to cool.

# cheddar and pepper muffins

### ingredients

250 g (8 oz) plain flour
1$\frac{1}{2}$ teaspoons baking powder
$\frac{1}{2}$ teaspoon bicarbonate of soda
$\frac{1}{2}$ teaspoon salt
$\frac{1}{4}$ teaspoon cayenne pepper
90 g (3 oz) polenta
250 g (8 oz) mature cheddar, grated
6-8 spring onions (green onions),
  green tops sliced thinly
1 small red capsicum (pepper), diced
4 tablespoons butter
2 tablespoons sugar
2 eggs
1$\frac{1}{4}$ cups (315 ml, 10 fl oz) buttermilk
**makes 18**

**1** Preheat oven to 220°C (425°F, gas mark 7). Into a large bowl, sift flour, baking powder, bicarbonate of soda, salt and cayenne pepper. Add polenta, cheddar, spring onions and capsicum and mix to combine.

**2** In a separate large bowl, beat butter and sugar until creamy, add eggs and beat until smooth. Fold dry ingredients into butter mixture alternately with buttermilk until just combined.

**3** Spoon batter into 18 greased $\frac{1}{3}$ cup (80 ml, 2$\frac{3}{4}$ fl oz) capacity muffin tins and bake for 15–18 minutes or until muffins are cooked when tested with a skewer. Turn onto wire racks to cool.

**i**

**preparation time**
20 minutes

**cooking time**
20 minutes

**nutritional value per serve**
fat: 12.7 g
carbohydrate: 23 g
protein: 9.5 g

1 Preheat oven to 200°C (400°F, gas mark 6). In a large bowl, combine flour, lemon thyme and paprika. In a separate bowl, whisk together egg, oil and milk. Add egg mixture to flour mixture and mix until just combined. Fold in the sardines. Spoon mixture into 12 lightly greased ½-cup (125 ml, 4 fl oz) muffin tins. Bake 12–15 minutes or until muffins are cooked when tested with a skewer. Turn onto wire racks to cool.

# mini sardine muffins

### ingredients

185 g (6 oz) self-raising flour
1 tablespoon roughly chopped lemon thyme
pinch paprika
1 egg
4 tablespoons vegetable oil
¾ cup (185 ml, 6 fl oz) milk
110 g (3½ oz) can sardines in tomato sauce, mashed
**makes 24**

i

**preparation time**
15 minutes

**cooking time**
15 minutes

**nutritional value per serve**
fat: 16.1 g
carbohydrate: 24 g
protein: 8.4 g

# sweet corn and cheese muffins

2 In a small bowl, whisk together egg, milk and butter. Pour milk mixture into the well in the flour mixture. Use a fork to mix ingredients until just combined.

3 Spoon mixture into 10 greased 1 cup (250 ml, 8 fl oz) capacity muffin tins. Bake for 20–30 minutes or until muffins are cooked when tested with a skewer. Turn onto wire racks to cool.

**i**

**preparation time**
20 minutes

**cooking time**
30 minutes

**nutritional value per serve**
fat: 9.3 g
carbohydrate: 27 g
protein: 7.2 g

## ingredients

250 g (8 oz) self-raising flour
$^1/_2$ teaspoon salt
315 g (10 oz) can corn kernels, drained
60 g (2 oz) cheddar, grated
2 tablespoons grated parmesan
1 egg, lightly beaten
$^3/_4$ cup (185 ml, 6 fl oz) milk
3 tablespoons butter, melted
extra butter for greasing
**makes 10**

1 Preheat oven to 180ºC (350ºF, gas mark 4). Into a large bowl, sift flour and salt. Add corn, cheddar and parmesan, and mix to combine. Make a well in the centre of flour mixture.

# basil-cheddar muffins

## ingredients

250 g (8 oz) plain flour
90 g (3 oz) cheddar, grated
1 tablespoon sugar
2¹/₂ teaspoons baking powder
¹/₄ teaspoon salt
90 g (3 oz) cream cheese
4 tablespoons chopped fresh basil
1 egg lightly beaten
³/₄ cup (185 ml, 6 fl oz) milk
4 tablespoons butter, melted
**makes 12**

**preparation time**
10 minutes

**cooking time**
50 minutes, plus
30 minutes
standing

**nutritional value
per serve**
fat: 16.9 g
carbohydrate: 28 g
protein: 9.1 g

1 Preheat oven to 200°C (400°F, gas mark 6). In a large bowl, combine flour, cheddar, sugar, baking powder and salt. Rub in cream cheese using fingertips until mixture resembles coarse breadcrumbs. Stir in basil. In a separate bowl, combine egg, milk and butter. Add to flour mixture, and mix until just combined.

2 Spoon batter into 12 greased ¹/₂ cup (125 ml, 4 fl oz) capacity muffin tins. Bake for 20–25 minutes or until muffins are cooked when tested with a skewer. Transfer to a wire rack to cool slightly. Serve warm.

# mushroom muffins

## ingredients

250 g (8 oz) plain flour
1 tablespoon baking powder
60 g (2 oz) mushrooms, chopped
110 g (3½ oz) brown rice
60 g (2 oz) mature cheddar, grated
1 tablespoon dried parsley
2 teaspoons chopped fresh chives
125 g (4 oz) butter, melted
1 cup (250 ml, 8 fl oz) milk
1 egg, beaten
**makes 12**

1 Preheat oven to 200°C (400°F, gas mark 6). Into a large bowl, sift flour and baking powder. Add mushrooms, rice, cheese, parsley and chives and mix to combine.

2 Make a well in the centre. Add the butter, milk and egg and mix until just combined.

3 Spoon mixture into lightly greased ½ cup (125 ml, 4 fl oz) capacity muffin tins and bake for 12–15 minutes or until muffins are cooked when tested with a skewer. Turn onto wire racks to cool.

**preparation time**
25 minutes

**cooking time**
12-15 minutes

**nutritional value
per serve**
fat: 15.1 g
carbohydrate: 31 g
protein: 7.5 g

# cheese and bacon muffins

## ingredients

4 rashers bacon, chopped
1 egg, lightly beaten
1 cup (250 ml, 8 fl oz) milk
4 tablespoons vegetable oil
2 tablespoons chopped fresh parsley
250 g (8 oz) self-raising flour, sifted
90 g (3 oz) mature cheddar, grated
butter for greasing
**makes 12**

i

**preparation time**
15 minutes

**cooking time**
25 minutes

**nutritional value
per serve**
fat: 14.7 g
carbohydrate: 22 g
protein: 10.8 g

**1** Preheat oven to 180°C (350°F, gas mark 4). Place bacon in a large frying pan and cook over a medium heat, stirring, until crisp. Remove and drain on kitchen paper. Set aside.

**2** In a large bowl, combine egg, milk, oil and parsley. Add flour and cheese and combine. Add bacon and mix until just combined.

**3** Spoon mixture into 12 greased ½ cup (125 ml, 4 fl oz) capacity muffin tins and bake for 20–25 minutes or until muffins are cooked when tested with a skewer. Turn onto wire racks to cool.

# tuscan herb muffins

## ingredients

250 g (8 oz) unbleached plain flour
1 tablespoon baking powder
1 teaspoon bicarbonate of soda
1/2 teaspoon salt
1 teaspoon dried oregano
1 teaspoon dried thyme
1 teaspoon dried basil
2 eggs
1 egg white
1 cup (250 ml, 8 fl oz) buttermilk
4 tablespoons olive oil
1 tablespoon honey
2 tablespoons grated parmesan
**makes 12**

**1** Preheat oven to 200°C (400°F, gas mark 6). In a large bowl, combine flour, baking powder, bicarbonate of soda, salt, oregano, thyme and basil. Set aside.

**2** In a separate large bowl, combine eggs, egg white, buttermilk, oil, honey and parmesan. Pour egg mixture into flour mixture, stirring until just combined.

**3** Pour mixture into 12 greased 1/2 cup (125 ml, 4 fl oz) capacity muffin tins and bake for 20–25 minutes or until muffins are cooked when tested with a skewer. Turn onto wire racks to cool.

_i_

**preparation time**
20 minutes

**cooking time**
25 minutes

**nutritional value
per serve**
fat: 12.5 g
carbohydrate: 30 g
protein: 7.6 g

# potato sour cream muffins

## ingredients

250 g (8 oz) mashed potato
2 eggs, lightly beaten
1 cup (250 ml, 8 fl oz) milk
³/₄ cup (185 ml, 6 fl oz) sour cream
4 tablespoons butter, melted
315 g (10 oz) self-raising flour, sifted
3 tablespoons snipped fresh chives

**makes 6**

**preparation time**
15 minutes

**cooking time**
30 minutes

**nutritional value per serve**

fat: 11.2 g
carbohydrate: 24 g
protein: 5.5 g

1 Preheat oven to 180°C (350°F, gas mark 4). In a large bowl, combine potatoes, eggs, milk, sour cream and butter.

2 In a separate bowl, combine flour and chives. Add to potato mixture and mix until just combined. Spoon mixture into 6 greased 1 cup (250 ml, 8 fl oz) capacity muffin tins and bake for 25–30 minutes or until muffins are cooked when tested with a skewer. Turn onto wire racks to cool.

# cheesy apple muffins

## ingredients

185 g (6 oz) wholemeal self-raising flour
$^1/_4$ teaspoon ground cinnamon
$^1/_4$ teaspoon ground nutmeg
$^1/_4$ teaspoon ground ginger
$^1/_4$ teaspoon ground cloves
1 teaspoon baking powder
45 g (1$^1/_2$ oz) oat bran
3 tablespoons brown sugar
1 green apple, peeled and grated
125 g (4 oz) ricotta
2 tablespoons vegetable oil
$^3/_4$ cup (185 ml, 6 fl oz) apple juice
**makes 12**

**i**

**preparation time**
10 minutes

**cooking time**
25 minutes

**nutritional value per serve**
fat: 7.3 g
carbohydrate: 26 g
protein: 5.5 g

**1** Preheat oven to 200°C (400°F, gas mark 6). Into a large bowl, sift flour, cinnamon, nutmeg, ginger, cloves and baking powder. Add oat bran and sugar, mix to combine.

**2** Make a well in the centre of the flour mixture. Stir in apple, ricotta, oil and apple juice and mix until just combined.

**3** Spoon mixture into lightly greased $^1/_2$ cup (125 ml, 4 fl oz) capacity muffin tins. Bake for 25 minutes or until muffins are cooked when tested with a skewer. Turn onto wire racks to cool.

# carrot and sesame muffins

## ingredients

375 g (12 oz) self-raising flour
1/2 teaspoon bicarbonate of soda
1 teaspoon ground mixed spice
90 g (3 oz) brown sugar
1 large carrot, grated
4 tablespoons sesame seeds, toasted
170 g (5 1/2 oz) sultanas
200 g (7 oz) natural yoghurt
1 cup (250 ml, 8 fl oz) milk
3 tablespoons butter, melted
3 egg whites, lightly beaten
**makes 24**

i

**preparation time**
15 minutes

**cooking time**
20 minutes

**nutritional value
per serve**
fat: 6.6 g
carbohydrate: 36 g
protein: 6 g

**1** Preheat oven to 200°C (400°F, gas mark 6). Into a large bowl, sift flour, bicarbonate of soda and mixed spice. Add sugar, carrot, sesame seeds and sultanas and mix to combine.

**2** In a large bowl, place yoghurt, milk, butter and egg whites and whisk to combine. Stir yoghurt mixture into flour mixture and mix until just combined. Spoon batter into lightly greased 1/2 cup (125 ml, 4 fl oz) capacity muffin tins and bake for 20 minutes or until muffins are cooked when tested with a skewer. Turn onto wire racks to cool.

# pumpkin muffins

## ingredients

165 g (5¹/₂ oz) plain flour
100 g (3¹/₂ oz) buckwheat flour
¹/₂ cup (125 g, 4 oz) sugar
1¹/₂ teaspoons baking powder
1 teaspoon ground cinnamon
¹/₂ teaspoon bicarbonate of soda
¹/₂ teaspoon salt
2 eggs, slightly beaten
250 g (8 oz) pumpkin, cooked
   and mashed
¹/₂ cup (125 ml, 4 fl oz) low-fat milk
2 tablespoons cooking oil
¹/₂ teaspoon grated orange rind (zest)
4 tablespoons orange juice
extra butter for greasing
**makes 12**

**1** Preheat oven to 200°C (400°F, gas mark 6). In a large bowl, combine flour, buckwheat flour, sugar, baking powder, cinnamon, bicarbonate of soda and salt. Make a well in the centre of flour mixture and set aside.

**2** In a separate bowl, combine eggs, pumpkin, milk, oil, orange rind and orange juice. Add to the flour mixture and mix until just combined.

**3** Spoon batter into 12 greased ¹/₂ cup (125 ml, 4 fl oz) capacity muffin tins. Bake for 15–20 minutes or until cooked when tested with a skewer. Cool in tins for 5 minutes. Transfer onto a wire rack to cool.

**i**

**preparation time**
15 minutes

**cooking time**
15-20 minutes

**nutritional value
per serve**
fat: 5.3 g
carbohydrate: 32 g
protein: 5.6 g

# classic blueberry muffins

## ingredients

- 315 g (10 oz) self-raising flour
- 1 teaspoon baking powder
- 90 g (3 oz) sugar
- 2 eggs, lightly beaten
- 1 cup (250 ml, 8 fl oz) buttermilk or milk
- 4 tablespoons butter, melted
- 155 g (5 oz) blueberries
- 1 tablespoon finely grated orange rind (zest)
- 2 tablespoons coffee sugar crystals or raw sugar
- extra butter for greasing

**makes 6**

**i**

**preparation time**
15 minutes

**cooking time**
30 minutes

**nutritional value per serve**
fat: 8.4 g
carbohydrate: 36 g
protein: 5.2 g

**1** Preheat oven to 200°C (400°F, gas mark 6). Into a large bowl, sift flour and baking powder. Add sugar and combine.

**2** In a separate bowl, combine eggs, milk and butter. Add egg mixture, blueberries and orange rind to flour mixture and mix until just combined.

**3** Spoon mixture into 6 greased 1 cup (250 ml, 8 fl oz) capacity muffin tins. Sprinkle with coffee sugar crystals or raw sugar and bake for 20–30 minutes or until muffins are cooked when tested with a skewer. Turn onto wire racks to cool.

# mango bran muffins

## ingredients

125 g (4 oz) self-raising flour
2 teaspoons baking powder
1 teaspoon ground cardamom
45 g (1½ oz) oat bran
4 tablespoons brown sugar
1 mango, chopped
2 egg whites
¾ cup (185 ml, 6 fl oz) low-fat milk
4 tablespoons vegetable oil

**makes 12**

**1** Preheat oven to 190°C (375°F, gas mark 5). Into a large bowl, sift flour, baking powder and cardamom. Add bran, sugar and mango and mix to combine.

**2** In a large bowl, place egg whites, milk and oil and whisk to combine. Stir milk mixture into flour mixture and mix well to combine.

**3** Spoon mixture into 12 nonstick ½ cup (125 ml, 4 fl oz) capacity muffin tins and bake for 15–20 minutes or until muffins are cooked when tested with a skewer. Turn onto a wire rack to cool.

**i**

**preparation time**
15 minutes

**cooking time**
20 minutes

**nutritional value per serve**
fat: 10.3 g
carbohydrate: 26 g
protein: 5 g

# spiced apple muffins

**1** Preheat oven to 200°C (400°F, gas mark 6). Line a muffin or deep bun tin with 9 muffin cases and set aside. In a large bowl, combine flour, baking powder, mixed spice and salt.

**2** In another large bowl, combine sugar, egg, milk and melted butter. Gently fold in the flour mixture until just combined – do not over handle. The mixture should be quite lumpy. Gently fold in apple.

## ingredients

200 g (7 oz) plain wholemeal flour
1 tablespoon baking powder
1 teaspoon ground mixed spice
pinch of salt
4 tablespoons brown sugar
1 medium egg, beaten
220 ml (7¹/₂ fl oz) low-fat milk
4 tablespoons butter
1 cooking apple, peeled, cored and chopped
**makes 9**

**i**

**preparation time**
20 minutes

**cooking time**
20 minutes

**nutritional value per serve**
fat: 9.1 g
carbohydrate: 29 g
protein: 6 g

**3** Divide mixture between the muffin cases. Bake in the oven for 20 minutes or until cooked when tested with a skewer. Transfer to a wire rack to cool.

# lemon poppy seed muffins

### ingredients

2 eggs, lightly beaten
1 cup (250 ml, 8 fl oz) sour cream
1/2 cup (125 ml, 4 fl oz) milk
4 tablespoons oil
4 tablespoons honey
3 tablespoons poppy seeds
1 tablespoon grated lemon rind (zest)
280 g (9 oz) self-raising flour, sifted
butter for greasing
*lemon cream cheese icing*
4 tablespoons cream cheese, softened
1 tablespoon lemon juice
125 g (4 oz) icing sugar
**makes 6**

1 Preheat oven to 180°C (350°F, gas mark 4). In a large bowl, combine eggs, sour cream, milk, oil, honey, poppy seeds and lemon rind.

2 Add flour to poppy seed mixture and mix until just combined.

3 Spoon mixture into 6 greased 1 cup (250 ml, 8 fl oz) capacity muffin tins and

bake for 25–30 minutes or until muffins are cooked when tested with a skewer. Turn onto wire racks to cool.

4 In a food processor, combine cream cheese, lemon juice and icing sugar until smooth. Top cooled muffins with icing.

i

**preparation time**
20 minutes

**cooking time**
30 minutes

**nutritional value per serve**
fat: 16.9 g
carbohydrate: 35 g
protein: 5.5 g

# choc rough muffins

## ingredients

125 g (4 oz) butter
1/2 cup (125 g, 4 oz) sugar
2 eggs, lightly beaten
250 g (8 oz) self-raising flour, sifted
4 tablespoons cocoa powder, sifted
175 g (5 1/2 oz) chocolate chips
45 g (1 1/2 oz) desiccated coconut
3/4 cup (185 ml, 6 fl oz) buttermilk
   or milk
makes 6

**preparation time**
15 minutes

**cooking time**
35 minutes

**nutritional value per serve**
fat: 19.4 g
carbohydrate: 40 g
protein: 6.7 g

1 Preheat oven to 180°C (350°F, gas mark 4). In a large bowl, place butter and sugar and beat until light and fluffy. Gradually beat in eggs.

2 In a separate bowl, combine flour and cocoa powder. Add flour mixture, chocolate chips, coconut and milk to butter mixture and mix until just combined.

3 Spoon mixture into 6 greased 1 cup (250 ml, 8 fl oz) capacity muffin tins and bake for 35 minutes or until muffins are cooked when tested with a skewer. Turn onto wire racks to cool.

# orange and blueberry muffins

## ingredients

1 orange
1/2 cup (125 ml, 4 fl oz) orange juice
125 g (4 oz) butter, chopped
1 egg
185 g (6 oz) plain flour
170 g (5 1/2 oz) castor sugar
1 teaspoon bicarbonate of soda
1 teaspoon baking powder
1/4 teaspoon salt
125 g (4 oz) blueberries
**makes 12-16**

1. Preheat oven to 200°C (400°F, gas mark 6). Peel rind (zest) from orange, remove all pith, cut rind into small pieces. Remove membrane and seeds from orange and cut into small segments.

2. In a food processor, place orange rind and segments, orange juice, butter and egg and process until well combined and mixture has curdled. Transfer mixture to a large bowl.

3. Into a separate bowl, sift flour, sugar, bicarbonate of soda, baking powder and salt. Add to orange mixture and mix lightly to combine. Batter should be lumpy. Fold in berries.

4. Divide batter between 12–16 greased 1/3 cup (90 ml, 3 fl oz) capacity muffin tins, filling two-thirds full. Bake for 18–20 minutes until cooked when tested with a skewer. Turn onto a wire rack to cool.

*i*

**preparation time**
20 minutes

**cooking time**
20 minutes

**nutritional value per serve**
fat: 11.9 g
carbohydrate: 36 g
protein: 3.2 g

# oat-bran fruit muffins

## ingredients

185 g (6 oz) self-raising flour
75 g (2¹/₂ oz) oat bran
95 g (3 oz) brown sugar
¹/₂ cup (125 ml, 4 fl oz) vegetable oil
2 eggs
85 g (3 oz) dried mixed fruit, chopped
1 cup (250 ml, 8 fl oz) buttermilk
**makes 12**

**1** Preheat oven to 190°C (375°F, gas mark 5). In a large bowl, combine flour, oat bran and brown sugar.

**2** In a separate bowl, whisk together oil and eggs and add to the dry ingredients. Add dried mixed fruit and buttermilk and mix until just combined.

**3** Spoon mixture into lightly greased ¹/₂ cup (125 ml, 4 fl oz) capacity muffin tins. Bake for 25–30 minutes until muffins are cooked when tested with a skewer. Turn onto wire racks to cool.

i

**preparation time**
15 minutes

**cooking time**
30 minutes

**nutritional value per serve**
fat: 15.7 g
carbohydrate: 35 g
protein: 5.9 g

# banana choc-chip muffins

**i**

**preparation time**
15 minutes

**cooking time**
20 minutes

**nutritional value
per serve**
fat: 15.3 g
carbohydrate: 38 g
protein: 4.8 g

## ingredients

1 large ripe banana, mashed
1 cup (250 ml, 8 fl oz) milk
1 egg
125 g (4 oz) butter, melted
185 g (6 oz) self-raising flour
125 g (4 oz) castor sugar
130 g (4½ oz) choc bits
**makes 12**

**1** Preheat oven to 190°C (375°F, gas mark 5). In a large bowl, combine banana, milk, egg and melted butter. Add flour, sugar and choc bits and mix until just combined.

**2** Spoon mixture into well-greased ½ cup (125 ml, 4 fl oz) capacity muffin tins. Bake for 20 minutes or until muffins are cooked when tested with a skewer. Turn onto wire racks to cool.

# apple & bran muffins

## ingredients

230 g (7 1/2 oz) wholemeal self-raising flour
1/2 teaspoon ground nutmeg
1/4 teaspoon baking powder
30 g (1 oz) wheat bran cereal, toasted
4 tablespoons brown sugar
2 green apples, grated
2 eggs, lightly beaten
3 tablespoons low-fat natural yoghurt
1 tablespoon vegetable oil
butter for greasing

**makes 12**

*i*

**preparation time**
15 minutes

**cooking time**
20 minutes

**nutritional value per serve**
fat: 4.4 g
carbohydrate: 30 g
protein: 5.9 g

1 Preheat oven to 180°C (350°F, gas mark 4). Into a large bowl, sift flour, nutmeg and baking powder. Add bran cereal and sugar and mix to combine.

2 Make a well in centre of flour mixture. Add apples, eggs, yoghurt and oil and mix until just combined.

3 Spoon mixture into 12 greased 1/2 cup (125 ml, 4 fl oz) capacity muffin tins and bake for 15 minutes or until muffins are cooked when tested with a skewer. Turn onto wire racks to cool.

# sticky date muffins

### ingredients

250 g (8 oz) self-raising flour
1 teaspoon bicarbonate of soda
1 teaspoon ground cinnamon
4 tablespoons brown sugar
90 g (3 oz) butter
125 g (4 oz) pitted dates, chopped
1 egg, lightly beaten
1 cup (250 ml, 8 fl oz) buttermilk or milk
*brandy sauce*
100 g (3½ oz) butter
3 tablespoons brown sugar
1 tablespoon golden syrup
1 tablespoon brandy
**makes 6**

**i**

preparation time
20 minutes

cooking time
35 minutes

nutritional value
per serve
fat: 16.2 g
carbohydrate: 40 g
protein: 4 g

**1** Preheat oven to 190°C (375°F, gas mark 5). Into a large bowl, sift flour, bicarbonate of soda and cinnamon. Set aside.

**2** Place 4 tablespoons sugar, 90 g (3 oz) butter and dates in a small pan and heat over a low heat, stirring constantly until butter melts. Pour date mixture into dry ingredients, add egg and milk. Mix until just combined.

**3** Spoon mixture into 6 greased 1 cup (250 ml, 8 fl oz) capacity muffin tins and bake for 30 minutes until muffins are cooked when tested with a skewer.

**4** Place remaining butter and sugar, golden syrup and brandy in a small pan and heat over a low heat, stirring constantly, until sugar dissolves. Bring to the boil, reduce heat and simmer for 3 minutes until sauce is thick and syrupy. Serve with warm muffins.

# maple-nut bran muffins

## ingredients

155 g (5 oz) firmly packed maple or brown sugar
60 g (2 oz) walnuts, finely chopped
2 tablespoons unbleached plain flour
1/2 teaspoon ground cinnamon
250 g (8 oz) wheat bran cereal
3/4 cup (185 ml, 6 fl oz) milk
1 egg
4 tablespoons butter, melted
1 cup (125 g, 4 oz) unbleached plain flour
2 1/2 teaspoons baking powder
1/2 teaspoon salt
125 g (4 oz) sugar
**makes 12**

i

**preparation time**
25 minutes &
20 minutes
soaking
**cooking time**
25 mins
**nutritional value
per serve**
fat: 12.5 g
carbohydrate: 50 g
protein: 6.9 g

1 Preheat oven to 200°C (400°F, gas mark 6). In a medium bowl combine maple or brown sugar, walnuts, flour and cinnamon. Set aside.

2 In a medium bowl, combine cereal and milk. Set aside for 20 minutes until most of the liquid is absorbed. Beat in egg and melted butter.

3 Into a large bowl, sift flour and baking powder. Add salt and sugar, and mix to combine. Add cereal mixture, combining until moistened. Spoon a small amount of batter into 12 greased 1/2 cup (125 ml, 4 fl oz) capacity muffin tins. Sprinkle with some of the filling. Repeat layers until tins are full.

4 Bake for 20–25 minutes or until muffins are cooked when tested with a skewer. Turn onto wire racks to cool.

# orange-raisin muffins

### ingredients

250 g (8 oz) unbleached plain flour
125 g (4 oz) sugar
1 tablespoon baking powder
1/2 teaspoon salt
60 g (2 oz) raisins
1 egg
1 cup (250 ml, 8 fl oz) milk
3 tablespoons butter, melted
2 teaspoons grated orange rind (zest)
**make 12**

**1** Preheat oven to 200°C (400°F, gas mark 6). In a large bowl, combine flour, sugar, baking powder, salt, and raisins. Make a well in the centre.

**2** In a medium bowl, beat egg, milk, melted butter and orange rind. Add egg mixture to flour mixture, stirring until just combined.

**3** Spoon mixture into 12 greased 1/2 cup (125 ml, 4 fl oz) capacity muffin tins. Bake for 20–25 minutes or until muffins are cooked when tested with a skewer. Turn onto wire racks to cool.

i

**preparation time**
15 minutes

**cooking time**
25 minutes

**nutritional value
per serve**
fat: 8 g
carbohydrate: 44 g
protein: 5.4 g

# mini chocolate muffins with mocha sauce

## ingredients

60g (2oz) unsalted butter, diced, plus
   extra for greasing
60g (2oz) plain cooking chocolate,
   roughly chopped
2 medium eggs
100 g (3½ oz) castor sugar
100 g (3½ oz) self-raising flour
30g (1oz) cocoa powder, sifted,
   plus extra for dusting

### mocha sauce

150g (5oz) plain chocolate, roughly
   chopped
90mL (3fl oz) espresso or other strong,
   good quality coffee
155mL (5oz) double cream

**makes 12**

**2** Spoon batter into 12 greased ½ cup (125 ml, 4 fl oz) capacity muffin tins. Bake for 15 minutes or until muffins are cooked when tested with a skewer. Turn onto wire racks to cool.

**3** Place the chocolate, coffee and 4 tablespoons of the cream into a small pan and heat gently. Simmer for 1–2 minutes, until sauce has thickened slightly. Keep warm.

**4** Allow muffins to cool on a wire rack for 5 minutes. Whisk remaining cream until thickened, spoon over the muffins along with the mocha sauce. Serve dusted with cocoa powder.

**1** Preheat oven to 180°C (350°F, gas mark 4). Melt chocolate and butter in a bowl set over a pan of simmering water. In a large bowl, place the eggs, sugar, flour and cocoa powder. Beat for 1 minute then fold in melted chocolate and butter.

**i**

**preparation time**
20 minutes

**cooking time**
25 minutes

**nutritional value
per serve**
fat: 23.9 g
carbohydrate: 36 g
protein: 5.8 g

# banana and pineapple muffins

## ingredients

185 g (6 oz) wholemeal self-raising flour
1 teaspoon baking powder
1 teaspoon mixed spice
4 tablespoons brown sugar
45 g (1½ oz) oat bran
1 small banana, mashed
150 g (5 oz) can crushed pineapple, drained
3 egg whites, lightly beaten
2 tablespoons vegetable oil
½ cup (125 ml, 4 fl oz) pineapple juice

**makes 12**

i

**preparation time**
20 minutes

**cooking time**
20 minutes

**nutritional value per serve**
fat: 5.7 g
carbohydrate: 30 g
protein: 5.6 g

**1** Preheat oven to 200°C (400°F, gas mark 6). Into a large bowl, sift flour, baking powder and spice. Add sugar and oat bran and mix to combine.

**2** Make a well in the centre of the flour mixture. In a separate bowl, combine banana, pineapple, egg whites, oil and juice. Stir into flour mixture and mix until just combined.

**3** Spoon mixture into lightly greased ½ cup (125 ml, 4 fl oz) capacity muffin tins. Bake for 12–15 minutes or until muffins are cooked when tested with a skewer. Turn onto wire racks to cool.

# carrot ginger muffins

## ingredients

250 g (8 oz) unbleached plain flour
1 tablespoon baking powder
1 teaspoon bicarbonate of soda
1/2 teaspoon salt
1/2 teaspoon ground nutmeg
1/2 teaspoon ground cinnamon
2 teaspoons freshly grated ginger
1/2 cup (125 ml, 4 fl oz) yoghurt or
   buttermilk
4 tablespoons vegetable oil
4 tablespoons maple syrup
4 tablespoons honey
3 eggs
310 g (10 oz) carrot, grated
**makes 12**

**i**

**preparation time**
20 minutes

**cooking time**
20 minutes

**nutritional value
per serve**
fat: 8.4 g
carbohydrate: 32 g
protein: 4.8 g

**1** Preheat oven to 200°C (400°F, gas mark 6). In a large bowl combine flour, baking powder, bicarbonate of soda, salt, nutmeg and cinnamon.

**2** In a separate bowl, combine ginger, yoghurt, oil, maple syrup, honey and eggs. Add egg mixture to flour mixture and mix to combine. Stir in carrots.

**3** Spoon mixture into greased 1/2 cup (125 ml, 4 fl oz) capacity muffin tins. Bake for 15–18 minutes or until muffins are cooked when tested with a skewer. Serve warm.

# blackberry spice muffins

## ingredients

75 g (2½ oz) self-raising wholemeal flour
60 g (2 oz) self-raising flour
½ teaspoon ground allspice
3 tablespoons brown sugar
60 g (2 oz) ground almonds
185 g (6 oz) blackberries
1 banana, mashed
1 cup (250 ml, 8 fl oz) buttermilk
⅓ cup (90 ml, 3 fl oz) vegetable oil
1 egg, lightly beaten

**makes 12**

i

**preparation time**
15 minutes

**cooking time**
25 minutes

**nutritional value per serve**
fat: 14.7 g
carbohydrate: 19 g
protein: 5.1 g

1 Preheat oven to 190°C (375°F, gas mark 5). Into a large bowl, sift wholemeal flour, flour and allspice. Return husks to bowl. Add sugar, almonds, blackberries and banana and mix to combine.

2 In a large bowl, place buttermilk, oil and egg and whisk to combine. Stir milk mixture into flour mixture and mix until just combined.

3 Spoon mixture into 12 greased ½ cup (125 ml, 4 fl oz) capacity muffin tins and bake for 15–20 minutes or until muffins are cooked when tested with a skewer. Turn onto a wire rack to cool.

# apricot oat bran muffins

## ingredients

250 g (8 oz) self-raising flour
1 teaspoon baking powder
45 g (1½ oz) oat bran
60 g (2 oz) dried apricots, chopped
60 g (2 oz) sultanas
1 egg, lightly beaten
1½ cups (325 ml, 12 fl oz) buttermilk
  or milk
2 tablespoons golden syrup
90 g (3 oz) butter, melted
extra butter for greasing
**makes 6**

**preparation time**
15 minutes

**cooking time**
20 minutes

**nutritional value**
**per serve**
fat: 10.3 g
carbohydrate: 34 g
protein: 5.8 g

1 Preheat oven to 180°C (350°F, gas mark 4). Into a large bowl, sift flour and baking powder. Add oat bran, apricots and sultanas, mix to combine and set aside.

2 In a small bowl, place egg, milk, golden syrup and butter and whisk to combine.

3 Add milk mixture to dry ingredients and mix until just combined. Spoon mixture into 6 greased 1 cup (250 ml, 8 fl oz) capacity muffin tins and bake for 15–20 minutes or until muffins are cooked when tested with a skewer. Turn onto wire racks to cool.

# cranberry-spice muffins

## ingredients

125 g (4 oz) fresh cranberries, coarsely chopped
125 g (4 oz) sugar
250 g (8 oz) unbleached plain flour
1 tablespoon baking powder
½ teaspoon salt
½ teaspoon ground cinnamon
¼ teaspoon ground nutmeg
1 egg
1 cup (250 ml, 8 fl oz) milk
3 tablespoons butter, melted
2 teaspoons grated orange rind (zest)

**makes 12**

**i**

**preparation time**
20 minutes

**cooking time**
25 minutes

**nutritional value per serve**
fat: 7.3 g
carbohydrate: 36 g
protein: 5.1 g

**1** Preheat oven to 200°C (400°F, gas mark 6). In a small bowl, combine cranberries and sugar. Set aside.

**2** In a large bowl, combine flour, baking powder, salt, cinnamon and nutmeg. Make a well in the centre. In a medium bowl, beat egg, milk, melted butter and orange rind. Pour egg mixture into flour mixture, stirring until just combined and with last few strokes add cranberry mixture.

**3** Spoon mixture into 12 greased ½ cup (125 ml, 4 fl oz) capacity muffin tins and bake for 20–25 minutes or until muffins are cooked when tested with a skewer. Turn onto wire racks to cool.

# lemon-currant muffins

### ingredients

2 teaspoons finely grated lemon rind (zest)
95 g (3 oz) brown sugar
250 g (8 oz) unbleached plain flour
4 tablespoons raw sugar
1 tablespoon baking powder
½ teaspoon salt
⅛ teaspoon ground nutmeg
4 tablespoons dried currants
1 egg
1 cup (250 ml, 8 fl oz) milk
3 tablespoons butter, melted
1 tablespoon finely grated lemon rind
1 tablespoon lemon juice
**makes 12**

**1** Preheat oven to 200°C (400°F, gas mark 6). In a small bowl, combine 2 teaspoons lemon rind and brown sugar. Mix well and set aside.

**2** In a large bowl, combine flour, raw sugar, baking powder, salt, nutmeg and currants. Make a well in the centre. In a medium bowl, beat the egg. Add milk, butter, lemon juice and remaining lemon rind. Pour egg mixture into flour mixture, stirring until just combined.

**3** Pour mixture into 12 greased ½ cup (125 ml, 4 fl oz) capacity muffin tins. Sprinkle evenly with lemon sugar and bake 20–25 minutes until muffins are cooked when tested with a skewer. Turn onto wire racks to cool.

i

**preparation time**
20 minutes

**cooking time**
25 minutes

**nutritional value per serve**
fat: 7.5 g
carbohydrate: 44 g
protein: 5.1 g

# scones

# scones

## ingredients

250 g (8 oz) self-raising flour
1 teaspoon baking powder
2 teaspoons sugar
3 tablespoons butter
1 egg
1/2 cup (125 ml, 4 fl oz) milk

**makes 12**

**1** Preheat oven to 220°C (425°F, gas mark 7). Into a large bowl, sift flour and baking powder. Stir in sugar, then rub in butter, using fingertips, until mixture resembles coarse breadcrumbs.

**i**

**preparation time**
15 minutes

**cooking time**
12-15 minutes

**nutritional value per serve**
fat: 11.8 g
carbohydrate: 38 g
protein: 7.1 g

**2** In a small bowl, whisk egg and milk. Make a well in the centre of flour mixture, pour in egg mixture and mix to form a soft dough. Turn onto a lightly floured surface and knead lightly.

**3** Press dough out to a 2 cm thickness, using palm of hand. Cut out scones using a floured 5 cm pastry cutter. Avoid twisting the cutter or the scones will rise unevenly.

**4** Arrange scones close together on a greased and lightly floured baking tray or in a shallow 20 cm-round cake tin. Brush with a little milk and bake for 12–15 minutes or until risen and golden.

# fresh strawberry scones

## ingredients

225 g (7½ oz) self-raising
wholemeal flour
1 teaspoon baking powder
pinch of salt
4 tablespoons butter
2 tablespoons castor sugar
100 g (3½ oz) fresh strawberries,
  chopped
½ cup (125 ml, 4 fl oz) low-fat milk
extra milk for glazing
**makes 12**

**preparation time**
15 minutes
**cooking time**
10-15 minutes
**nutritional value
per serve**
fat: 12.2 g
carbohydrate: 32 g
protein: 6.1 g

**1** Preheat oven to 220°C (425°F, gas mark 7). In a large bowl, place flour, baking powder and salt and mix to combine. Lightly rub in the butter with fingertips until the mixture resembles breadcrumbs.

**2** Add sugar, strawberries and enough milk to form a soft dough. Turn the dough out onto a floured surface, knead lightly, then carefully roll to a thickness of 2 cm.

**3** Cut out 12 rounds, using a 5-cm pastry cutter, and place side by side on a baking sheet. Brush with milk to glaze. Bake for 8–10 minutes, until risen and golden brown. Transfer to a wire rack to cool.

# pumpkin scones

## ingredients

4 tablespoons butter
2 tablespoons castor sugar
125 g (4 oz) pumpkin, cooked and mashed
1/4 teaspoon nutmeg
1 egg
1/2 cup (125 ml, 4 fl oz) milk
285 g (9 oz) self-raising flour, sifted

**makes 12**

i

**preparation time**
15 minutes

**cooking time**
20 minutes

**nutritional value per serve**
fat: 10.9 g
carbohydrate: 34 g
protein: 5.7 g

1 Preheat oven to 210°C (415°F, gas mark 6–7). In a large bowl, cream butter and sugar until well combined. Add pumpkin and nutmeg and mix well. Add egg, then gradually add milk. Stir in sifted flour and gently mix to a soft dough.

2 Turn dough onto a floured surface and knead lightly, then carefully roll to a thickness of 2½ cm. Cut out 12 rounds using a 5 cm pastry cutter.

3 Place onto a greased baking sheet and brush with milk to glaze. Bake for 15–20 minutes until risen and golden brown. Transfer to a wire rack to cool. Serve with butter.

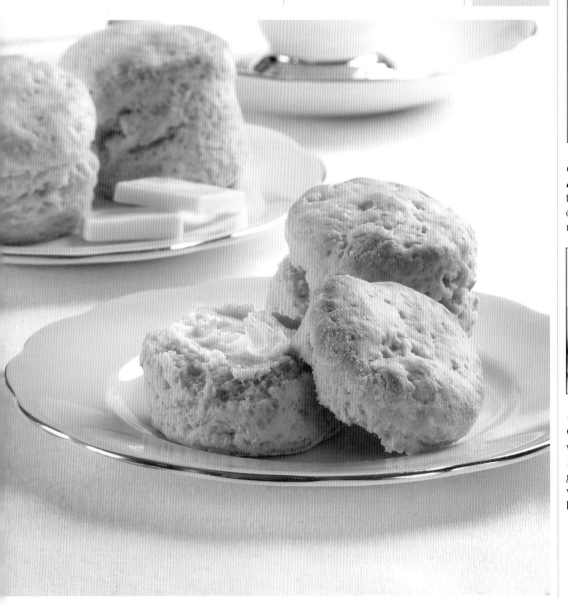

# fresh herb and oat scones

## ingredients

185 g (6 oz) self-raising flour, sifted
45 g (1½ oz) instant oats
½ teaspoon baking powder
2 tablespoons butter
2 teaspoons chopped fresh parsley
2 teaspoons chopped fresh basil
2 teaspoons chopped fresh rosemary
¾ cup (190 ml, 6 fl oz) skim milk
**makes 9**

1 Preheat oven to 220°C (425°F, gas mark 7). In a large bowl, place flour, oats and baking powder. Rub in butter using fingertips until mixture resembles fine breadcrumbs. Stir in parsley, basil and rosemary.

2 Make a well in the centre of the mixture and pour in milk. Mix lightly with a knife until all ingredients are just combined. Turn mixture out onto a lightly floured board and knead lightly.

3 Gently roll dough out evenly to 2 cm thickness. Cut into rounds using a 5 cm floured pastry cutter. Arrange side by side in a lightly greased 18 cm round shallow baking tin. Brush tops with a little extra milk and bake for 15–20 minutes or until risen and golden. Turn onto a wire rack to cool.

**i**

**preparation time**
20 minutes

**cooking time**
20 minutes

**nutritional value
per serve**
fat: 7.9 g
carbohydrate: 35 g
protein: 6.7 g

# cheddar and apple scones

## ingredients

4 tablespoons butter, cubed,
extra butter for greasing
210 g (7 oz) self-raising flour
1 teaspoon baking powder
salt
60 g (2 oz) fine oatmeal
extra oatmeal for dusting
1 teaspoon english mustard powder
1 teaspoon light muscovado sugar
125 g (4 oz) cheddar, cubed
1 large eating apple, peeled, cored and
    chopped into pieces
4-5 tablespoons sour cream or buttermilk
extra sour cream or buttermilk for glazing
**makes 10–12**

**1** Preheat oven to 200°C (400°F, gas mark 6). Grease a large baking sheet.

**2** Into a large bowl, sift the flour, baking powder and a good pinch of salt, stir in oatmeal, mustard powder and sugar. Rub in the butter using your fingertips until it resembles fine breadcrumbs. Fold in the cheese and apples and add just enough sour cream or buttermilk to make a soft but not sticky dough.

**3** Turn dough out onto a floured surface and lightly roll to a thickness of 2 cm and cut out 10–12 scones, using a

6 cm pastry cutter. Place on the baking sheet, brush the tops with soured cream or buttermilk and lightly dust with oatmeal. Bake for 10–12 minutes until well risen and golden. Transfer to a wire rack to cool.

*i*

**preparation time**
20 minutes

**cooking time**
15 minutes

**nutritional value
per serve**
fat: 18.5 g
carbohydrate: 27 g
protein: 7.6 g

# potato scones

## ingredients

185 g (6 oz) plain flour
1 teaspoon baking powder
½ teaspoon salt
125 g (4 oz) butter
2 eggs, beaten
100 ml (3½ fl oz) milk
125 g (4 oz) cooked but cold potato, finely mashed
3 shallots, finely chopped
ground black pepper
extra flour, for kneading
extra butter, for spreading

**serves 6-8**

*i*

**preparation time**
15 minutes

**cooking time**
30 minutes

**nutritional value per serve**
fat: 18.3 g
carbohydrate: 23 g
protein: 6.2 g

**1** Preheat oven to 230°C (450°F, gas mark 8). Into a large bowl, sift flour, baking powder and salt. Rub in butter using fingertips until it resembles coarse breadcrumbs. In a separate bowl, beat eggs and milk. Add to flour mixture to make a soft dough.

**2** Add mashed potatoes, shallots and pepper. Knead through lightly. Turn onto a floured board, lightly knead, then roll out to 1 cm thickness. Cut into rounds using a 2.5 cm pastry cutter. Bake for 30 minutes or until golden and risen.

**3** Split open while hot, spread with butter and serve.

# cheese and onion scones

### ingredients

500 g (1 lb) self-raising flour
1 teaspoon salt
1/4 teaspoon cayenne pepper
4 tablespoons butter
100 g (3 1/2 oz) cheddar, grated
1 tablespoon finely chopped parsley
1 tablespoon finely chopped onion
1 egg, beaten
1 1/2 cups (375 ml, 12 fl oz) milk

**serves 6**

**1** Preheat oven to 230°C (450°F, gas mark 8). Into a large bowl, sift flour, salt and cayenne pepper. Rub butter into flour using fingertips until it resembles coarse breadcrumbs. Add cheese, parsley and onion and mix to combine.

**2** Make a well in the centre, add egg and milk, and mix

quickly to a soft dough. Turn out onto a floured board and knead lightly.

**3** Gently roll to 1 cm thickness and cut into 5 cm rounds using a pastry cutter. Place on a floured tray and brush with milk. Bake for 10–15 minutes or until scones are golden and firm.

**i**

**preparation time**
20 minutes

**cooking time**
15 minutes

**nutritional value per serve**
fat: 10.8 g
carbohydrate: 32 g
protein: 8.3 g

# quick breads

# mini savoury croissants

### ingredients

250 g (8 oz) prepared puff pastry
1 egg
1 tablespoon water
butter for greasing

**asparagus and cheese filling**
60 g (2 oz) gruyère cheese, grated
4 fresh asparagus spears, blanched and finely chopped
1/4 teaspoon ground paprika
black pepper
**makes 12**

*i*

**preparation time**
20 minutes

**cooking time**
15-20 minutes

**nutritional value per serve**
fat: 19 g
carbohydrate: 21 g
protein: 8.7 g

**1** Preheat oven to 200°C (400°F, gas mark 5). In a large bowl, combine cheese, asparagus, paprika and black pepper to taste.

**2** Roll out pastry to 0.3 cm-thick and cut into 10 cm-wide strips. Cut each strip into triangles with 10 cm edge at the base.

**3** Place a little filling across the base of each triangle, roll up from the base and mould into a croissant shape. In a small bowl, lightly beat egg with water then brush over croissant.

**4** Place croissants on greased baking trays and bake for 12–15 minutes or until puffed and golden. Serve hot or cold.

# basil-beer bread

## ingredients

375 g (12 oz) self-raising flour, sifted
4 tablespoons sugar
30 g (1 oz) chopped fresh basil
1 teaspoon crushed black peppercorns
1¹/₂ cups (375 ml, 12 fl oz) beer, at room
temperature

**makes 1**

**1** Preheat oven to 160°C (315°F, gas mark 2–3). In a large bowl, combine flour, sugar, basil, peppercorns and beer to make a soft dough.

**2** Place dough in a greased and lined 11 x 21 cm loaf tin and bake for 50 minutes or until bread is cooked when tested with a skewer.

**3** Stand bread in tin for 5 minutes before turning onto a wire rack to cool. Serve warm or cold.

**preparation time**
20 minutes

**cooking time**
50 minutes

**nutritional value
per serve**
fat: 0.6 g
carbohydrate: 39 g
protein: 4.5 g

# cheese and bacon damper

## ingredients

310 g (10 oz) self-raising flour
3 tablespoons butter
2 teaspoons dried parsley flakes
1 teaspoon chopped fresh chives
250 g (8 oz) mature cheddar, grated
2 rashers cooked bacon, finely chopped
1 egg
$^{3}/_{4}$ cup (185 ml, 6 fl oz) milk
**serves 6–8**

*i*

**preparation time**
20 minutes

**cooking time**
30–40 minutes

**nutritional value
per serve**
fat: 16.9 g
carbohydrate: 24 g
protein: 13.5 g

**1** Preheat oven to 180°C (350°F, gas mark 4). Into a large bowl, sift flour. Rub in butter using your fingertips, until mixture resembles coarse breadcrumbs. Stir in parsley, chives, cheese and bacon, and mix well to combine.

**2** In a separate bowl, combine the egg and milk. Stir into flour mixture and mix to a soft dough. Turn dough onto a lightly floured board and knead lightly.

**3** Shape into a cob and cut a deep cross in the centre. Place on a sheet of baking paper on an oven tray. Bake for 30 minutes or until risen and golden.

# blue cheese and walnut damper

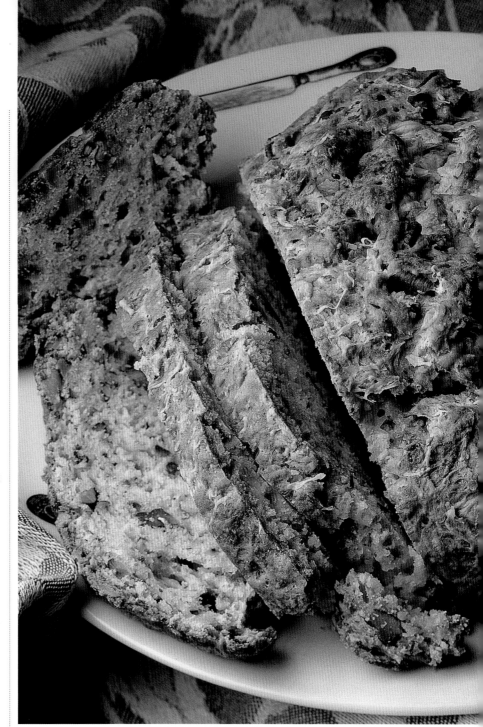

## ingredients

310 g (10 oz) self-raising flour, sifted
220 g (7¹/₂ oz) blue cheese, crumbled
1 tablespoon snipped fresh chives
1 teaspoon paprika
155 g (5 oz) walnuts, chopped
1 cup (250 ml, 8 fl oz) buttermilk or milk
1 tablespoon walnut or vegetable oil
60 g (2 oz) parmesan, grated
**makes 1**

**1** Preheat oven to 180°C (350°F, gas mark 4). In a large bowl, combine flour, blue cheese, chives, paprika and 125 g (4 oz) walnuts.

**2** Make a well in the centre of flour mixture, add milk and oil and mix to form a soft dough.

**3** Turn dough onto a lightly floured surface and knead until smooth. Roll into a large ball, flatten slightly and place on a lightly greased baking tray. Sprinkle with parmesan and remaining walnuts. Bake for 40 minutes or until golden and risen.

**i**

**preparation time**
20 minutes

**cooking time**
40 minutes

**nutritional value per serve**
fat: 22.4 g
carbohydrate: 22 g
protein: 12.6 g

# sun-dried tomato and provolone quick bread

## ingredients

4 tablespoons olive oil
2 tablespoons sugar
2 large eggs
2 cloves garlic, crushed
1¼ cups (185 ml, 6 fl oz) buttermilk
375 g (12 oz) unbleached bread flour
2 teaspoon baking powder
½ teaspoon bicarbonate of soda
1½ teaspoons salt
125 g (4 oz) provolone or other sharp
   yellow cheese, grated
60 g (2 oz) spring onions (green
   onions), thinly sliced
30 g (1 oz) fresh parsley, chopped
1 teaspoon freshly ground black pepper
80 g (3 oz) sun-dried tomatoes, chopped
**serves 4-6**

1 In a large bowl, combine the oil, sugar, eggs, garlic and buttermilk until smooth.

2 In a separate bowl, combine the flour, baking powder, bicarbonate of soda and salt, then add cheese, spring onions, parsley, pepper and tomatoes.

3 Add the buttermilk mixture to the flour mixture and stir until just combined.

4 Pour the batter into a greased 20 cm x 10 cm loaf tin, smooth top with a wet spoon and bake for 50 minutes or until risen and golden. Allow to cool for 10 minutes before removing from tin.

i

**preparation time**
25 minutes

**cooking time**
50 minutes

**nutritional value
per serve**
fat: 12.4 g
carbohydrate: 31 g
protein: 9.7 g

# olive soda bread

## ingredients

125 g (4 oz) butter, softened
4 tablespoons sugar
1 egg
450 g (14 oz) wholemeal self-raising flour
185 g (6 oz) plain flour
1¹/₂ teaspoons bicarbonate of soda
1¹/₂ cups (375 ml, 12 fl oz) buttermilk
  or milk
125 g (4 oz) pitted black olives, chopped
2 teaspoons dried fennel seeds
1 teaspoon coarse sea salt
**makes 1**

### i

**preparation time**
20 minutes

**cooking time**
45 minutes

**nutritional value per serve**
fat: 9.9 g
carbohydrate: 37 g
protein: 6.8 g

1 Preheat oven to 200°C (400°F, gas mark 6). In a food processor, place butter, sugar and egg and process until smooth. Add wholemeal flour, plain flour, bicarbonate of soda and milk and process to form a soft dough.

2 Turn dough onto a lightly floured surface and knead in olives. Shape dough into a 20 cm round and place on a lightly greased and floured baking tray.

3 Using a sharp knife, cut a cross in the top. Sprinkle with fennel seeds and salt and bake for 45 minutes or until golden and firm.

# shortbread

**preparation time**
20 minutes

**cooking time**
25 minutes

**nutritional value
per serve**
fat: 25.3 g
carbohydrate: 55 g
protein: 5.7 g

## ingredients

200 g (7 oz) butter, softened
125 g (4 oz) castor sugar
1 teaspoon vanilla essence
280 g (9 oz) plain flour, sifted
60 g (2 oz) rice flour, sifted
**makes 1**

**1** 1 Preheat oven to 160°C (315°F, gas mark 2–3). In a large bowl, place butter, sugar and vanilla essence and beat until light and fluffy. Add flour and rice flour and mix to combine.

**2** Turn dough onto a lightly floured surface and roll out to form a 2 cm-thick circle.

**3** Pinch edges or press dough into a large shortbread mould. Place on a lightly greased baking tray and bake for 25 minutes or until lightly browned.

# pumpkin spice loaf

## ingredients

185 g (6 oz) unbleached plain flour
125 g (4 oz) oatmeal or oat flour
2 teaspoons baking powder
2 teaspoons bicarbonate of soda
2 teaspoons ground cinnamon
2 teaspoons ground nutmeg
1/4 teaspoon allspice
2 teaspoons grated fresh ginger
1/2 cup (125 ml, 4 fl oz) maple syrup
4 tablespoons molasses
4 tablespoons butter, melted
2 egg whites
1 egg
2 tablespoons lemon juice
1 tablespoon grated orange rind (zest)
250 g (8 oz) pumpkin, cooked and mashed
**makes 1**

**i**

**preparation time**
20 minutes

**cooking time**
1 hour

**nutritional value per serve**
fat: 6.6 g
carbohydrate: 38 g
protein: 4.6 g

**1** Preheat oven to 180°C (350°F, gas mark 4). In a large bowl, combine flour, oatmeal, baking powder, bicarbonate of soda, cinnamon, nutmeg and allspice. Make a well in the centre.

**2** In a separate large bowl, combine remaining ingredients. Add to the flour mixture and mix until combined.

**3** Pour mixture into a well greased 20 x 10 cm loaf tin. Bake for 50–60 minutes until golden and risen. Cool in tin for 10 minutes. Turn onto a wire rack to cool.

# easy berry bread

### ingredients

375 g (12 oz) self-raising flour
1¹/₂ teaspoons ground mixed spice
1 teaspoon baking powder
1¹/₂ tablespoons sugar
2 tablespoons butter
¹/₂ cup (125 ml, 4 fl oz) water
¹/₂ cup (125 ml, 4 fl oz) milk
200 g (7 oz) fresh raspberries
1 tablespoon castor sugar
1 tablespoon milk

**makes 1**

**preparation time**
20 minutes

**cooking time**
30 minutes

**nutritional value
per serve**
fat: 5.2 g
carbohydrate: 40 g
protein: 5.5 g

1 Preheat oven to 220°C (425°F, gas mark 7). Into a large bowl, sift flour, mixed spice and baking powder. Add sugar then, using your fingertips, rub in butter until mixture resembles coarse breadcrumbs.

2 Make a well in the centre of flour mixture and, using a round-ended knife, mix in water and milk to form a soft dough.

3 Turn dough onto a floured surface and knead lightly until smooth. Divide dough into two portions and flatten each into an 18 cm round.

4 Sprinkle raspberries and sugar over surface of one round leaving 2.5 cm around edge. Brush edge with a little milk and place remaining round on top. Seal edges securely using fingertips.

5 Place on a greased and lightly floured baking tray. Brush surface of loaf with a little milk and bake for 10 minutes. Reduce oven temperature to 180°C (350°F, gas mark 4) and bake for a further 20–25 minutes until golden and risen.

# blueberry pecan loaf

## ingredients

250 g (8 oz) unbleached plain flour
2 teaspoon baking powder
1/2 teaspoon salt
1/4 teaspoon bicarbonate of soda
1/4 teaspoon ground nutmeg
125 g (4 oz) sugar
60 g (2 oz) pecans, chopped
2 eggs
4 tablespoons milk
1/2 cup (125 ml, 4 fl oz) orange juice
2 teaspoons grated orange rind (zest)
90 g (3 oz) butter, melted
155 g (5 oz) blueberries

**makes 1**

ℹ

**preparation time**
25 minutes

**cooking time**
65-70 minutes

**nutritional value
per serve**
fat: 13.2 g
carbohydrate: 33 g
protein: 5 g

**1** 1 Preheat oven to 180°C (350°F, gas mark 4). In a large bowl combine flour, baking powder, salt, bicarbonate of soda, nutmeg and sugar. Mix in pecans. Make a well in the centre.

**2** In a medium bowl, beat eggs with milk, orange juice and rind. Fold in melted butter. Add egg mixture to flour mixture, mixing until just combined. Gently fold in blueberries.

**3** Pour batter into a well greased 20 x 10 cm loaf tin. Bake for 55–65 minutes until loaf is golden and risen. Cool in pan for 10 minutes. Turn onto a wire rack to cool.

# lemon quick bread

## ingredients

125 g (4 oz) butter, softened
125 g (4 oz) sugar
2 large eggs, beaten
grated rind (zest) and juice of 1 lemon
$^1/_4$ teaspoon cinnamon
$^1/_2$ teaspoon ground coriander
225 g (7$^1/_2$ oz) unbleached bread flour
$^1/_2$ teaspoon salt
2 teaspoon baking powder
$^1/_2$ cup (125 ml, 4 fl oz) milk
**serves 4**

1 Preheat oven to 180ºC (350ºF, gas mark 4). In a large bowl, cream the butter and sugar until light and fluffy. Add the eggs, one at a time, beating well after each addition. Add lemon rind and juice, cinnamon and coriander. Mix well.

2 In a large bowl, combine the flour, salt and baking powder.

3 Add half of the flour mixture and half of the milk to the butter mixture, fold together, add remaining flour and milk and fold again until combined.

4 Pour into a greased baking pot and bake for 45 minutes or until cooked when tested with a skewer. Cool in the pot for 10 minutes. Turn onto a wire rack to cool.

i

**preparation time**
20 minutes

**cooking time**
45 minutes

**nutritional value per serve**
fat: 15.6 g
carbohydrate: 37 g
protein: 5.5 g

# hot-cross buns

## ingredients

60 g (2 oz) skim milk powder
1 cup (250 ml, 8 fl oz) warm water
75 g (2½ oz) sugar
90 g (3 oz) butter, melted
2 tablespoons dried yeast
500 g (1 lb) plain flour
1 teaspoon salt
1 teaspoon ground cinnamon
1 teaspoon mixed spice
1 tablespoon gluten powder
5 tablespoons currants
4 tablespoons sultanas
1 tablespoon mixed peel

*cross batter:*
3 tablespoons plain flour
3 teaspoons castor sugar
water to mix

*bun glaze:*
½ cup (125 ml, 4 fl oz) water
125 g (4 oz) sugar

**makes 16**

1 Preheat oven to 230°C (450°F, gas mark 8). In a large bowl, dissolve milk powder in warm water. Add ⅓ cup of sugar, butter and yeast. Into another large bowl, sift 4 cups of flour, salt, spices and gluten. Pour the yeast mixture over dry ingredients, mix well to form a soft dough – adding extra warm water if necessary.

**preparation time**
1 hour

**cooking time**
30 minutes

**nutritional value per serve**
fat: 7.8 g
carbohydrate: 68 g
protein: 8.3 g

2 Knead mixture thoroughly on a floured board for 10 minutes or until smooth.

3 Place dough in a greased bowl, cover with a tea towel and stand in a warm place for about 45 minutes until mixture doubles in size. Knead the currants and sultanas into the dough. Shape the dough into 16 buns and place in a greased deep-sided large baking dish. Stand in a warm place for a further 15–20 minutes.

4 In a bowl, combine flour and castor sugar, adding enough water to give a cream like consistency. Using this batter, pipe crosses on each bun.

5 Bake for 15 minutes or until buns are golden and firm. Place remaining sugar and water in a small saucepan, stir over low heat until sugar has dissolved. Simmer for 5 minutes without stirring. Brush buns with glaze while hot. Transfer onto wire racks to cool.

# french honey-spice bread

## ingredients

155 g (5 oz) almonds, coarsely chopped
60 g (2 oz) sultanas
$1/2$ teaspoon salt
$1/4$ teaspoon ground nutmeg
$1/2$ teaspoon ground anise seed
$1/2$ teaspoon ground ginger
1 teaspoon ground cinnamon
pinch ground cloves
2 teaspoons grated orange rind (zest)
1 teaspoon baking powder
2 teaspoons bicarbonate of soda
1 cup (250 ml, 8 fl oz) water
1 cup (250 ml, 8 fl oz) honey
4 tablespoons brown sugar
1 egg, lightly beaten
$1/3$ cup (80 ml, $2^3/4$ fl oz) dark rum
100 g ($3^1/2$ oz) rye flour
125 g (4 oz) bread flour
**makes 1**

**1** Preheat oven to 200°C (400°F, gas mark 6). In a large bowl, combine almonds, raisins, salt, nutmeg, anise, ginger, cinnamon, cloves, orange rind, baking powder and bicarbonate of soda. Set aside.

*i*

**preparation time**
25 minutes

**cooking time**
40 minutes

**nutritional value per serve**
fat: 9.4 g
carbohydrate: 56 g
protein: 6.5 g

**2** In a medium pan, bring water to the boil. Add honey and sugar and stir until sugar is dissolved. Remove from heat and allow to stand for 5 minutes. Add egg and rum to honey-sugar mixture and whisk to combine. Add to spice mixture and stir to combine. Add rye, wholemeal and bread flours and mix until just combined.

**3** Pour batter into a prepared 20 x 10 cm loaf tin and bake 10 minutes. Reduce heat to 180°C (350°F, gas mark 4) and bake a further 30 minutes until golden and risen. Cool in tin for 5 minutes. Turn onto a wire rack to cool.

# chocolate chip orange bread

### ingredients

250 g (8 oz) unbleached plain flour
2 teaspoons baking powder
¹/₂ teaspoon salt
¹/₄ teaspoon bicarbonate of soda
125 g (4 oz) sugar
60 g (2 oz) chopped walnuts
150 g (5 oz) chocolate chips
2 eggs
4 tablespoons milk
¹/₂ cup (125 ml, 4 fl oz) orange juice
2 teaspoons grated orange rind (zest)
1 teaspoon vanilla extract
90 g (3 oz) butter, melted
**makes 1**

**i**

**preparation time**
20 minutes

**cooking time**
1 hour

**nutritional value
per serve**
fat: 17.1 g
carbohydrate: 41 g
protein: 6.5 g

**1** Preheat oven to 180°C (350°F, gas mark 4). In a large bowl, combine flour, baking powder, salt, bicarbonate of soda and sugar. Add walnuts and ³/₄ cup of the chocolate chips, mix to combine. Make a well in the centre.

**2** In a medium bowl, beat eggs with milk, orange juice, orange rind and vanilla. Fold in butter. Pour egg mixture into flour mixture, mixing until just combined.

**3** Pour batter into a well greased 20 x 10 cm loaf tin. Sprinkle evenly with remaining chocolate chips. Bake for 55–60 minutes until golden and risen. Cool in tin for 10 minutes. Turn onto a wire rack to cool.

# apricot banana bread

## ingredients

250 g (8 oz) unbleached plain flour
1 teaspoon baking powder
½ teaspoon bicarbonate of soda
½ teaspoon salt
250 g (8 oz) sugar
125 g (4 oz) dried apricots, chopped
60 g (2 oz) walnuts, chopped
1 egg
½ cup (125 ml, 4 fl oz) milk
1 tablespoon walnut oil
1 tablespoon oil
1 ripe banana, mashed
**makes 1**

**i**

**preparation time**
25 minutes

**cooking time**
70 minutes

**nutritional value
per serve**
fat: 9 g
carbohydrate: 50 g
protein: 5.3 g

**1** Preheat oven to 180°C (350°F, gas mark 4). In a large bowl, combine flour, baking powder, bicarbonate of soda, salt and sugar. Add apricots and walnuts, mix to combine. Make a well in the centre.

**2** In a medium bowl, beat the egg with milk and oils. Fold in banana. Add banana mixture to flour mixture, stirring until just combined.

**3** Pour batter into a well greased 20 x 10 cm loaf tin. Bake for 65–70 minutes until loaf is well browned. Cool in tin for 10 minutes. Turn onto a wire rack to cool.

# gingerbread people

### ingredients

125 g (4 oz) butter
90 g (3 oz) brown sugar
1 egg yolk
310 g (10 oz) plain flour
1 teaspoon bicarbonate of soda
3 teaspoons ground ginger
2$^1/_2$ tablespoons golden syrup
**makes 20**

**1** Preheat oven to 180°C (350°F, gas mark 4). In a large bowl, cream butter and brown sugar until light and fluffy. Beat in the egg yolk, mixing well.

**2** In a separate bowl, sift flour and bicarbonate of soda. Gradually fold into creamed mixture, along with golden syrup. Knead lightly to form a soft dough.

**3** Divide dough into small portions. Roll out each portion to a thickness of $^1/_2$ cm between two sheets of greaseproof paper. Cut out small gingerbread shapes using a gingerbread man pastry cutter or hand shape with a small sharp knife. Place on lightly greased oven trays. Bake for 10 minutes. Transfer to wire racks to cool.

**preparation time**
20 minutes

**cooking time**
10-15 minutes

**nutritional value per serve**

fat: 18.1 g
carbohydrate: 58 g
protein: 6.1 g

# glossary

**al dente:** Italian term to describe pasta and rice that are cooked until tender but still firm to the bite.

**bake blind:** to bake pastry cases without their fillings. Line the raw pastry case with greaseproof paper and fill with raw rice or dried beans to prevent collapsed sides and puffed base. Remove paper and fill 5 minutes before completion of cooking time.

**baste:** to spoon hot cooking liquid over food at intervals during cooking to moisten and flavour it.

**beat:** to make a mixture smooth with rapid and regular motions using a spatula, wire whisk or electric mixer; to make a mixture light and smooth by enclosing air.

**beurre manié:** equal quantities of butter and flour mixed together to a smooth paste and stirred bit by bit into a soup, stew or sauce while on the heat to thicken. Stop adding when desired thickness results.

**bind:** to add egg or a thick sauce to hold ingredients together when cooked.

**blanch:** to plunge some foods into boiling water for less than a minute and immediately plunge into iced water. This is to brighten the colour of some vegetables; to remove skin from tomatoes and nuts.

**blend:** to mix 2 or more ingredients thoroughly together; do not confuse with blending in an electric blender.

**boil:** to cook in a liquid brought to boiling point and kept there.

**boiling point:** when bubbles rise continually and break over the entire surface of the liquid, reaching a temperature of 100°C (212°F). In some cases food is held at this high temperature for a few seconds then heat is turned to low for slower cooking. See simmer.

**bouquet garni:** a bundle of several herbs tied together with string for easy removal, placed into pots of stock, soups and stews for flavour. A few sprigs of fresh thyme, parsley and bay leaf are used. Can be purchased in sachet form for convenience.

**caramelise:** to heat sugar in a heavy-based pan until it liquefies and develops a caramel colour. Vegetables such as blanched carrots and sautéed onions may be sprinkled with sugar and caramelised.

**chill:** to place in the refrigerator or stir over ice until cold.

**clarify:** to make a liquid clear by removing sediments and impurities. To melt fat and remove any sediment.

**coat:** to dust or roll food items in flour to cover the surface before the food is cooked. Also, to coat in flour, egg and breadcrumbs.

**cool:** to stand at room temperature until some or all heat is removed, eg, cool a little, cool completely.

**cream:** to make creamy and fluffy by working the mixture with the back of a wooden spoon, usually refers to creaming butter and sugar or margarine. May also be creamed with an electric mixer.

**croutons:** small cubes of bread, toasted or fried, used as an addition to salads or as a garnish to soups and stews.

**crudite:** raw vegetable sticks served with a dipping sauce.

**crumb:** to coat foods in flour, egg and breadcrumbs to form a protective coating for foods which are fried. Also adds flavour, texture and enhances appearance.

**cube:** to cut into small pieces with six even sides, eg, cubes of meat.

**cut in:** to combine fat and flour using 2 knives scissor fashion or with a pastry blender, to make pastry.

**deglaze:** to dissolve dried out cooking juices left on the base and sides of a roasting dish or frying pan. Add a little water, wine or stock, scrape and stir over heat until dissolved. Resulting liquid is used to make a flavoursome gravy or added to a sauce or casserole.

**degrease:** to skim fat from the surface of cooking liquids, eg, stocks, soups, casseroles.

**dice:** to cut into small cubes.

**dredge:** to heavily coat with icing sugar, sugar, flour or cornflour.

**dressing:** a mixture added to completed dishes to add moisture and flavour, eg, salads, cooked vegetables.

**drizzle:** to pour in a fine thread-like stream moving over a surface.

**egg wash:** beaten egg with milk or water used to brush over pastry, bread dough or biscuits to give a sheen and golden brown colour.

**essence:** a strong flavouring liquid, usually made by distillation. Only a few drops are needed to flavour.

**fillet:** a piece of prime meat, fish or poultry which is boneless or has all bones removed.

**flake:** to separate cooked fish into flakes, removing any bones and skin, using 2 forks.

**flame:** to ignite warmed alcohol over food or to pour into a pan with food, ignite then serve.

**flute:** to make decorative indentations around the pastry rim before baking.

**fold in:** combining of a light, whisked or creamed mixture with other ingredients. Add a portion of the other ingredients at a time and mix using a gentle circular motion, over and under the mixture so that air will not be lost. Use a silver spoon or spatula.

**glaze:** to brush or coat food with a liquid that will give the finished product a glossy appearance, and on baked products, a golden brown colour.

**grease:** to rub the surface of a metal or heatproof dish with oil or fat, to prevent the food from sticking.

**herbed butter:** softened butter mixed with finely chopped fresh herbs and re-chilled. Used to serve on grilled meats and fish.

**hors d'ouvre:** small savoury foods served as an appetiser, popularly known today as 'finger food'.

**infuse:** to steep foods in a liquid until the liquid absorbs their flavour.

**joint:** to cut poultry and game into serving pieces by dividing at the joint.

**julienne:** to cut some food, eg, vegetables and processed meats into fine strips the length of matchsticks. Used for inclusion in salads or as a garnish to cooked dishes.

**knead:** to work a yeast dough in a pressing, stretching and folding motion with the heel of the hand until smooth and elastic to develop the gluten strands. Non-yeast doughs should be lightly and quickly handled as gluten development is not desired.

**line:** to cover the inside of a baking tin with paper for the easy removal of the cooked product from the baking tin.

**macerate:** to stand fruit in a syrup, liqueur or spirit to give added flavour.

**marinade:** a flavoured liquid, into which food is placed for some time to give it flavour and to tenderise. Marinades include an acid ingredient such as vinegar or wine, oil and seasonings.

**mask:** to evenly cover cooked food portions with a sauce, mayonnaise or savoury jelly.

**pan-fry:** to fry foods in a small amount of fat or oil, sufficient to coat the base of the pan.

**parboil:** to boil until partially cooked. The food is then finished by some other method.

**pare:** to peel the skin from vegetables and fruit. Peel is the popular term but pare is the name given to the knife used; paring knife.

**pith:** the white lining between the rind and flesh of oranges, grapefruit and lemons.

**pit:** to remove stones or seeds from olives, cherries, dates.

**pitted:** the olives, cherries, dates etc, with the stone removed, eg, purchase pitted dates.

**poach:** to simmer gently in enough hot liquid to almost cover the food so shape will be retained.

**pound:** to flatten meats with a meat mallet; to reduce to a paste or small particles with a mortar and pestle.

**simmer:** to cook in liquid just below boiling point at about 96°C (205°F) with small bubbles rising gently to the surface.

**skim:** to remove fat or froth from the surface of simmering food.

**stock:** the liquid produced when meat, poultry, fish or vegetables have been simmered in water to extract the flavour. Used as a base for soups, sauces, casseroles etc. Convenience stock products are available.

**sweat:** to cook sliced onions or vegetables, in a small amount of butter in a covered pan over low heat, to soften them and release flavour without colouring.

# conversions

measurements differ from country to country, so it's important to understand what the differences are. This Measurements Guide gives you simple 'at-a-glance' information for using the recipes in this book, wherever you may be.

Cooking is not an exact science – minor variations in measurements won't make a difference to your cooking.

### equipment

There is a difference in the size of measuring cups used internationally, but the difference is minimal (only 2–3 teaspoons). We use the Australian standard metric measurements in our recipes:

**1 teaspoon ....5 ml**  **1 tablespoon....20 ml**
**½ cup......125 ml**  **1 cup.....250 ml**
**4 cups...1 litre**

Measuring cups come in sets of one cup (250 ml), ½ cup (125 ml), ⅓ cup (80 ml) and ¼ cup (60 ml). Use these for measuring liquids and certain dry ingredients.
Measuring spoons come in a set of four and should be used for measuring dry and liquid ingredients.
When using cup or spoon measures always make them level (unless the recipe indicates otherwise).

### dry versus wet ingredients

While this system of measures is consistent for liquids, it's more difficult to quantify dry ingredients. For instance, one level cup equals: 200 g of brown sugar; 210 g of castor sugar; and 110 g of icing sugar.

When measuring dry ingredients such as flour, don't push the flour down or shake it into the cup. It is best just to spoon the flour in until it reaches the desired amount. When measuring liquids use a clear vessel indicating metric levels.

Always use medium eggs (55–60 g) when eggs are required in a recipe.

## dry

| metric (grams) | imperial (ounces) |
|---|---|
| 30 g | 1 oz |
| 60 g | 2 oz |
| 90 g | 3 oz |
| 100 g | 3½ oz |
| 125 g | 4 oz |
| 150 g | 5 oz |
| 185 g | 6 oz |
| 200 g | 7 oz |
| 250 g | 8 oz |
| 280 g | 9 oz |
| 315 g | 10 oz |
| 330 g | 11 oz |
| 370 g | 12 oz |
| 400 g | 13 oz |
| 440 g | 14 oz |
| 470 g | 15 oz |
| 500 g | 16 oz (1 lb) |
| 750 g | 24 oz (1½ lb) |
| 1000 g (1 kg) | 32 oz (2 lb) |

## liquids

| metric (millilitres) | imperial (fluid ounces) |
|---|---|
| 30 ml | 1 fl oz |
| 60 ml | 2 fl oz |
| 90 ml | 3 fl oz |
| 100 ml | 3½ fl oz |
| 125 ml | 4 fl oz |
| 150 ml | 5 fl oz |
| 190 ml | 6 fl oz |
| 250 ml | 8 fl oz |
| 300 ml | 10 fl oz |
| 500 ml | 16 fl oz |
| 600 ml | 20 fl oz (1 pint)* |
| 1000 ml (1 litre) | 32 fl oz |

*Note: an American pint is 16 fl oz.

### oven
Your oven should always be at the right temperature before placing the food in it to be cooked. Note that if your oven doesn't have a fan you may need to cook food for a little longer.

### microwave
It is difficult to give an exact cooking time for microwave cooking. It is best to watch what you are cooking closely to monitor its progress.

### standing time
Many foods continue to cook when you take them out of the oven or microwave. If a recipe states that the food needs to 'stand' after cooking, be sure not to overcook the dish.

### can sizes
The can sizes available in your supermarket or grocery store may not be the same as specified in the recipe. Don't worry if there is a small variation in size—it's unlikely to make a difference to the end result.

| cooking temperatures | °C (celsius) | °F (fahrenheit) | gas mark |
| --- | --- | --- | --- |
| very slow | 120 | 250 | 1/2 |
| slow | 150 | 300 | 2 |
| moderately slow | 160 | 315 | 2-3 |
| moderate | 180 | 350 | 4 |
| moderate hot | 190 | 375 | 5 |
| | 200 | 400 | 6 |
| hot | 220 | 425 | 7 |
| very hot | 230 | 450 | 8 |
| | 240 | 475 | 9 |
| | 250 | 500 | 10 |

# index